LITTLE SPARTA

THE GARDEN OF IAN HAMILTON FINLAY

JESSIE SHEELER

Photographs by Andrew Lawson

LITTLE SPARTA
THE GARDEN OF IAN HAMILTON FINLAY

JESSIE SHEELER

Photographs by Andrew Lawson

Frances Lincoln Ltd
4 Torriano Mews
Torriano Avenue
London NW5 2RZ
www.franceslincoln.com

Little Sparta
Copyright © Frances Lincoln Ltd 2003
Text copyright © Jessie Sheeler 2003
Photographs copyright © Andrew Lawson 2003

First Frances Lincoln edition: 2003

A catalogue record for this book is available from
the British Library.

ISBN 0 7112 2085 9

Designed by Becky Clarke

Printed and bound in China

2 3 4 5 6 7 8 9

Weathered brick and old stone blocks provide a
platform for ceramic capitals placed as planters
beside the camouflaged raspberry bed.

CONTENTS

ACKNOWLEDGEMENTS

Sue Swan and Pia Simig have worked most closely with Ian Hamilton Finlay in the creation of the garden, and Ralph Irving's work as gardener has contributed to its beauty. Artists and craftsmen who have carried out works in the garden described in this book include Maxwell Allen, John Andrew, Keith Bailey, David Ballantyne, John Brazenall, Gary Breeze, Jim Brennan, Keith Brookwell, Vincent Butler, Carving Workshop, Peter Coates, Ron Costley, Andrew Daish, David Edwick, Susan Goodricke, Peter Grant, Richard Grasby, Charles Gurrey, Christopher Hall, Michael Harvey, Gary Hincks, Celia Kilner, Richard Kindersley, John R. Nash, Richard Phethean, John Sellman, Nicholas Sloan, Alexander Stoddart, George Thompson, Andrew Townsend and Andrew Whittle. My thanks to Harry Gilonis for sharing his erudite insights with me, to Andrew Lawson whose idea this book was and whose photographs capture the spirit of the garden so well, and to Ian Hamilton Finlay for the pleasure and enrichment his work has brought me.

LITTLE FIELDS   LONG HORIZONS
LITTLE FIELDS LONG   FOR HORIZONS
HORIZONS LONG   FOR LITTLE FIELDS

The wordplay on 'long' is heightened by the wide landscape and the confinement suggested by the wall 'excerpts'.

Originally the only garden at Stonypath was in front of the house; the old currant bushes still flank the central path. The big ash tree at the foot of the Front Garden, old now and stripped of its great branches, was the only tree here when the Finlays arrived. The digging of the ponds and lochan provided a focus for the development of the land beyond the house and the English Parkland is the latest part to be tamed. Work is still in progress.

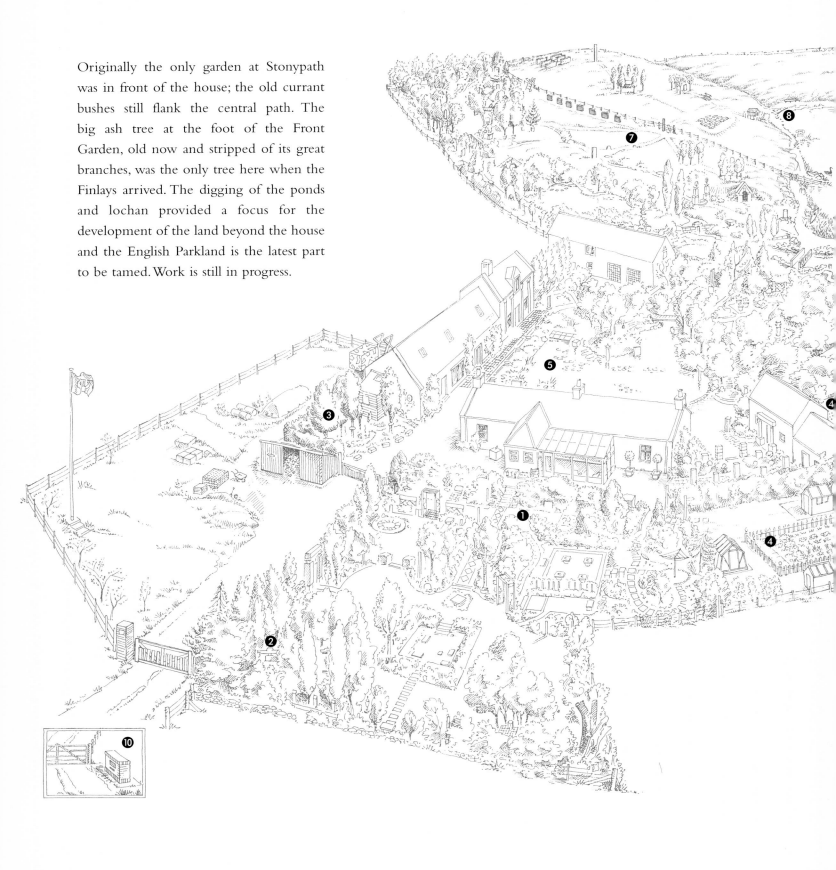

THE GARDEN

DRAWN BY GARY HINCKS

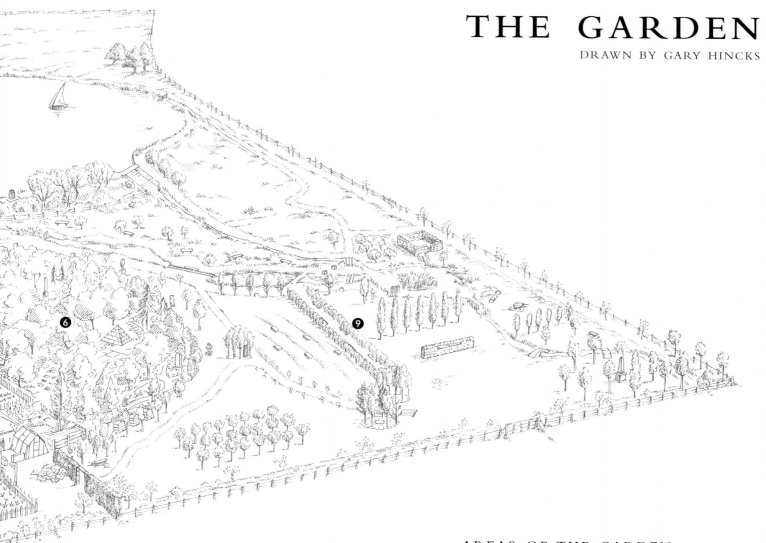

AREAS OF THE GARDEN

1. The Front Garden
2. The Roman Garden
3. Julie's Garden
4. The Allotment
5. The Temple Pool Garden
6. The Woodland Garden
7. The Wild Garden
8. Lochan Eck Garden
9. The English Parkland
10. Memorial to the First Battle of Little Sparta

PLEASE DO
NOT FEED
THE BOATS

INTRODUCTION

Above Regatta in the new pond, 1967. Eck Finlay's boat shows the home port letters SH – Stonypath.
Left Ian Hamilton Finlay beside the new pond, 1968. The building behind him became the Temple of Apollo.

To visit the poet–artist Ian Hamilton Finlay's garden at Stonypath in the Pentland Hills just south of Edinburgh is to arrive at a hidden oasis of fruitfulness and refreshment, not because the surrounding landscape is flat, barren or ugly – indeed the ever-changing play of light and gloom on the long vistas of high fields and moors is one of Scotland's lesser-known beauties. But Little Sparta, as it is now called, is a *hortus conclusus* within which the natural elements of plants, water, stone and earth have been transformed by the mind and hand of an artist into a place of inspirational beauty which presents the visitor with physical manifestations of moral truth, devotion to ideals and compassionate affection for what is simple and pure in our world. It is a garden of ideas and poetry, with works in stone, wood and metal almost invariably incorporating words, and set in surroundings which enhance or are actually part of the whole work, so that trees and bushes, running water and still ponds, grass and flowers become more significant by their appointment to a place within the artistic scheme. Finlay's method in creating the huge variety of his works is to collaborate with many other artists and craftsmen of the highest calibre in order to realize the works he conceives and designs in exact detail. Although the practice of an artist employing assistants or collaborators is an old and well-established one, it is hard to think of a body of work such as Finlay's, both at Little Sparta and in the worldwide locations of his other work, which is so consistently and successfully founded on the idea of co-operation. Little Sparta, the most extensive single collection of his work, is itself an art work, a paradox of fragility and indelible achievement, and certainly one of the most important art works made in contemporary Europe.

Although it has a timeless air of perfection now, not even half a century has passed since Stonypath was a bleak and empty place. In the autumn of 1966 this semi-derelict farm was a cold, weatherbeaten huddle of ruinous outbuildings beside the old farm cottage, with a muddy and overgrown midden in the yard between. The track leading up the hill from the Dunsyre road was indeed a stony path, rutted and tumbled by rain and the hooves of sheep and cattle. The fields and the surrounding moorland were windswept and bare. Stonypath was the neglected remnant of a hard, hill-farming life which had gone from it. Ian Hamilton Finlay's arrival marked the beginning of a transformation from stark, untended landscape into a unique art work.

The early years of Finlay's life were dramatic. He was born in 1925 to Scottish parents in the Bahamas where his father ran bootleg rum by schooner into Prohibition America. At the startlingly early age of six he was sent back to Scotland to boarding school, initially to Larchfield School in Helensburgh. There he had two memorable contacts with high culture, first being taught English by the poet W.H. Auden and secondly playing hide and seek with one of his school friends, a day boy whose home was wonderfully suited to the game – Hill House, built by Charles Rennie Mackintosh. In a move to a larger school, he proceeded to the rather more traditionally Scottish atmosphere of Dollar Academy where he remained until the abolition of the Prohibition laws put an end to his father's first enterprise. His parents moved to Florida and bought an orange grove which was promptly ruined by a hard and unseasonable frost, forcing their return to Scotland to start a new, impoverished life in Glasgow. They brought their son home to live with them and continue his education at the Albert Road Academy. However, before the Clydeside bombing of the Second World War began Ian was taken from home again, evacuated to the village of Gartmore, happily to a welcoming and comforting family. Here the world of heathery hills, peat-brown burns and the pleasures of fishing in them enchanted and absorbed him so that memories of those times reverberate in his early poems and stories.

Back in Glasgow in his mid-teens he knew he wanted to be an artist, and wrote to Herbert Read, probably the most influential critic of modern art writing in Britain from the thirties till his death in the sixties, earnestly asking advice as a young aspirant hoping to attend the Glasgow School of Art. Sadly – or perhaps fortunately – he received no reply and, though he did briefly study at the Art School, he soon decided to leave formal training behind and hitchhike to London with his girl friend, Marion. Their last lift south was in the back of a munitions lorry, with the intriguing result that he entered wartime London sitting on a torpedo. His time there brought him into contact with the literary and artistic life of Soho pubs, where his meetings with two Scottish artists, the two Roberts, Colquhoun and MacBryde, fed his passion for art.

After army service in Germany at the end of the war and further spells in London and Glasgow he and Marion married in a Glasgow register office. Finlay's best man was Christopher Grieve, better known as Hugh McDiarmid, at that time working on a ship based on the Clyde and later to become a vociferous literary enemy of Finlay's work. The Finlays went to live on the Orkney island of Rousay, then in the Perthshire hills near Comrie, where he was employed as a shepherd while he and Marion pursued their real work as artists. This was the period of his life during which he produced a series of paintings, now lost, and also wrote most of his short plays, broadcast by the BBC, and stories which appeared in the *Glasgow Herald*.

When his relationship with Marion broke down he moved to Edinburgh and eventually got a job as an advertising copywriter. This was not the ideal situation for a man who knew that his life should be that of an artist and lived in the country, not the city. The next move was back to Rousay, where the sea and its fishing boats were added to his mental stock of significant images, and life was sustained by working as a roadman. Painting, drawing and printmaking continued to form a part of his work over the next twenty years or so, as he went on writing plays for stage and radio, short stories and poems. It was in this work that he began to develop the disciplined, innovative brevity of expression and deeply allusive content which became the hallmark of his art.

In 1958 he published *The Sea Bed and Other Stories*, then in 1961 *The Dancers Inherit the Party*, a collection of short poems, both with cover illustrations by Zelko Kujundzic. Already the visual form of his work was important – the illustrations were the visually beautiful element in the literary art works. In 1961, during his stay in Edinburgh,

he co-founded the Wild Hawthorn Press, initially publishing the work of poets such as Louis Zukofsky and Lorine Neidecker but slowly making it into the publishing arm for his own increasingly prolific work. In the same year, from the more short-lived Wild Flounder Press, he produced a collection of poems in the Glasgow dialect, based on the classical Japanese *tanka* form of brief verses of a syllable pattern set in a way which grew naturally from the speech patterns of the language. *Glasgow Beasts an a Burd Haw an Inseks an Aw a Fush* suggested even more explicitly (and jokily) the possibilities of amalgamating word and image. In the early sixties his writing became more and more purely poetic while it shed reliance on syntax and he began to write what was essentially concrete poetry. This had been developing particularly in South American countries like Brazil and in mainland Europe, where the poet Eugen Gomringer was active. Concrete in the sense of being put together, composed of words as blocks of meaning not necessarily joined by narrative or program-matic connections, this poetry lays out on the page an image which elicits from the reader an imaginative response to the visual appearance of the words, the ideas they present and the juxtapositions of sound, shape or reference designed by the poet. His commitment to this way of writing allowed Finlay to explore the symbolic and visual properties of words, and develop a way of combining their appearance and meanings in works to be meditated upon as, say, a sculpture may be. At the same time, in the commodious hall cupboard of an Edinburgh New Town flat, he began to make painted wooden 'toys' – rocking boats, strings of drying fish, windmills – which embody the same iconic quality he was achieving with words.

In 1964 he met Sue Swan, or Finlay, with whom he then lived until the nineties. Together they moved to Ardgay in Easter Ross, to Gledfield Farmhouse, a square white house with a pine wood behind and a river beyond. Their first child, Eck, was born there and slept in a white

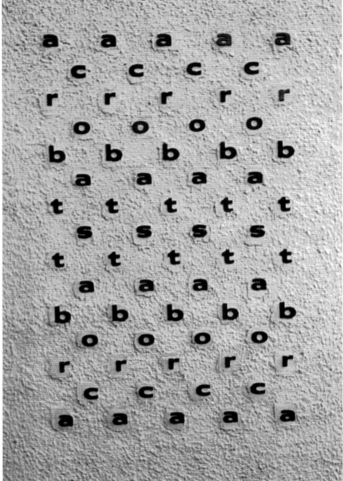

Suprematist cradle made by his father, under a knitted patchwork coverlet made by his mother. At Gledfield Finlay began to produce toys on a larger scale, and his first works made for a landscape were installed. Large painted wooden fish – an Orkney memory – are hung out to dry between the iron arms of a disused agricultural machine. A windsock in the form of an open-mouthed fish is caught on a straining line. Concrete poems made of coloured cork letters are stuck on the white harled walls of the house as in the cheerful *happy apple* and *acrobats*, where the eye gradually picks out the swinging acrobatic movements along the lines of repeated letters.

Placed on the rising slope of the garden, a wooden structure with V-shaped arms sticking up like windmill sails – or hare's ears – has words incorporated below:

THE HORIZON OF HOLLAND IS ALL EARS

From Gledfield the family moved briefly to the tiny Fife village Coaltown of Callange, where the first of Finlay's concrete poems sandblasted on glass were made. Words and the letters making them were the image, as in

WAVE ROCK

where the wave disintegrates into its constituent letters over the solid rock. But the cottage at Coaltown was desperately small and with great relief the Finlays moved to Stonypath where their daughter, Ailie, was born. Every place Finlay had made his home until then, every landscape and way of life, had been stored away in his heart as much as his head, building the great library of thought and image to be drawn on in his work. It was at Stonypath that time and space were to give him the opportunity to

Above An Arcadian ammunition dump, part of the defences put in place during the Little Spartan War.

conjure from the moorland hillside a work of art unprecedented in its nature and scope.

For the first few years every new idea was brought to fruition by sheer sweated labour. The Finlays moved old paving stones from the steadings, heaved boulders from one site to another, mixed concrete and cast it, laid brick paths, dug virgin moorland, cut wild grass and scrub to tame the landscape, planted trees, transplanted native ferns and flowers and found new ways to provide ground cover, spurred on by Sue Finlay's imaginative skill in choosing plants. Most amazingly of all, Finlay dug out enormous hollows in the hillside to make ponds and a lochan fed by

a single stream which ran down the hillside. They began the work of transforming the old farm buildings into a temple precinct which became the centre of an artist's garden, renewing the tradition of gardening as an exemplar of creative intellect: the Greek philosopher Epicurus cultivated a little vegetable garden to demonstrate his ideal of the quiet, productive life; the poet Alexander Pope created a garden at his home in Twickenham in accordance with his ideas of a good society; William Shenstone, the eighteenth-century 'man of taste' and inventor of the term 'landscape gardening', developed his estate at Leasowes in Shropshire to give substance to his theories of contrived 'natural' vistas including streams and winding paths.

The garden at Stonypath gradually took shape. The Temple, dedicated to Apollo, god of music, prophecy and archery, housed works brought together to form a sacred centre of meditation. Finlay's idea of the garden as a sanctuary of intellectual discipline and beauty gained strength, and in 1980 he renamed the garden Little Sparta, distinguishing his territory from that of the Athens of the North and honouring the uncompromising ideals of the Greek city state. The militaristic nature of that state had its place too in the concept of Little Sparta, following the Little Spartan War, which began in the late seventies. This sustained campaign arose from a dispute with the Scottish Arts Council over certain actions taken by its employees. Finlay withdrew a planned exhibition from the Scottish Arts Council gallery in protest and relations between the two parties broke down. Strathclyde Regional Council, at that time his Local Authority, then withdrew rates relief from the Temple on the grounds first that it was not supported by a grant from the Scottish Arts Council, and subsequently that it did not qualify for the normal rates exemption accorded to religious buildings. Finlay maintained that the culturally important question at issue was what defined a religious building in contemporary society, but Strathclyde refused to entertain discussion on this point, blocking any legal avenues of redress. Finlay promptly mustered a force of supporters for the cause, named the Saint-Just Vigilantes after the French Revolutionary leader, and in the First Battle of Little Sparta, 4 February 1983, the Vigilantes successfully defeated an attempt by the Sheriff's Officer to seize works from the Temple. Two weeks later in the Budget Day Raid, when the nation's attention was deflected to Westminster, Strathclyde's officer returned and succeeded in removing several works, most of which have never been returned although some were the property of artists, art collectors or institutions outwith Little Sparta. The first work to be seen today, set beside the track leading to Little Sparta, is the Memorial to the First Battle of Little Sparta. The bronze plaque shows a machine gun and the words

FLUTE, BEGIN WITH ME ARCADIAN NOTES

VIRGIL, ECLOGUE VIII

FEBRUARY 4 1983

Such combination of the pastoral, classical and polemical is a recurrent motif in the garden and immediately invites speculation. The barrel sleeve vents of the machine gun are equivalents for the finger stops of a flute; Arcady is the semi-mythical land of pastoral idyll peopled by hardy shepherds whose music and song enliven their days, celebrated in the poetry of Theocritus and Virgil. The metaphor linking machine-gun fire and flute melody underlines the interdependence of art and its defence. Conflict as a necessary circumstance for creativity can be seen as a founding principle in Little Sparta, from the very struggle to overcome the wildness of nature by the order of art.

William Shenstone's essay 'Unconnected Thoughts on Gardening' prompted Finlay's 'More Detached Sentences in the Manner of Shenstone'. One such Sentence defines the work of the artist: 'Gardening activity is of five kinds, namely, sowing, planting, fixing, placing, maintaining. In so far as gardening is an Art, all these may be taken under the one head, composing.' Taking this in conjunction with his maxim 'Look at what is there', applied to manipulating or changing the planting and natural architecture of the land available to him, an understanding of the relationship between the living elements of the garden, the artefacts and the ideas informing them becomes clearer. At every stage his placing of poetic works into the landscape has been accomplished in such a way as to make the garden elements as much part of the art work as the objects added to them. It is not a garden with art works in it, rather a cumulative and complicated work of art as a whole.

Certain themes, metaphors and images recur in the garden: the Second World War, the French Revolution, sea-fishing, pre-Socratic philosophy, romantic love, Western landscape painting, classical mythology. Works are imbued with wit, moral fervour and meditative thought, and the visitor passing from one part of the garden to another is gradually drawn into the reflective response that any great work of art elicits. A delightful and distinctive characteristic of Finlay's work is its recurrent affectionate humour –

follow a wooden signpost with the inscription *Zur Siegfried-Linie* and you will find yourself looking at the Stonypath washing line as you remember the Second World War soldiers' song making fun of the German defensive line in Western Europe: 'We're going to hang out our washing on the Siegfried Line . . .' Look carefully among the summer leaves and flowers in the Front Garden and you will notice two larger-than-life fibreglass tortoises, with *Panzer Leader* in Germanic script on their shells. The ruthlessly threatening and unstoppable German tank forces are enlisted to commemorate two real tortoises, family pets, which turned out to be highly aggressive and successful in their garden ravages! A hare, frequent visitor to (and nibbler of) the garden, known and loved by the Finlay children as well as their parents, is buried in the Woodland Garden with a stone marking its grave:

HIC LEPUSCULUS NOSTER
REQUIESCIT
QUI TESTUDINEM EXSPECTET
COWPER   AUGUST 1974

The dignified Latin inscription tells us 'Here rests our little Hare, waiting for the Tortoise', so the Scottish hare assumes the status of the Aesopian and takes his name from the English pastoral poet who also had a pet hare. The juxtaposition of the tender and the challenging, the intellectual and the emotional, the serious and the playful underlies the special nature of Little Sparta.

The garden's summer fruits are protected from guerrilla raids by subtle methods of camouflage: a network of poles in raspberry-red and leaf-green deceive eye, beak and hand, while strawberries have the double protection of tall wooden markers painted in green, strawberry-pink and cream with blue fishing net thrown over them. The blue of the net evokes both the summer sky above the ripe strawberries and the sea where the net might in another existence have gathered its harvest of fish, as the tumbling leaves of the plants recall the breaking waves. The words painted on the markers are *Strawberry camouflage* and *Fête des fraises*,

a phrase recalling the French Revolutionary festivals organized to honour such concepts as Virtue, Labour and Rewards.

In the English Parkland there is a work which suggests the essence of Little Sparta: *Inter Artes et Naturam* – 'Between Art and Nature'. It is a trellised pergola built to form a crossroads and made partly from stripped but unshaped branches and partly from clean planed planks. So Art is seen transforming the raw roughness of Nature, offering a contrast and a refinement to the eye as the visitor moves through the pergola, choosing a way at the crossing and coming out into the open garden where the tension between Art and Nature is everywhere demonstrated.

TRANSITIONS

A garden which has been created and enlarged over many years as Little Sparta has encompasses such different elements as glades, allées, thickets, waterways and enclosures, and there is a special pleasure in making the transition from one element or aspect to another. Often the transition is marked by a construction, as a sentence is marked by punctuation, bringing a pause in the rhythm of one's progress.

At the end of the track leading up through the fields Little Sparta is entered by a wide wooden gate. As it swings shut, a carved inscription on the inner side catches the eye.

das gepflügte Land • the fluted land

Beyond the gate and the enclosed garden the landscape through which the visitor has come stretches away. The fields and hills, the sheep, the curlews and skylarks and the ever-changing light on the Scottish pastoral are given description by the words on the gate as a painting might be given a title on its frame. This landscape is celebrated as that of classical poetry was by its imagined shepherds' flutes, and in some seasons, when the fields are ploughed and their cleared surface thus fluted in the manner of a Doric column, the metaphor acquires an added aspect.

Turning away from the entrance the visitor comes next to a smaller gateway into the old Front Garden of the farm cottage. Constructed from brick and stone piers with a

wooden gate, it carries an inscription on its outer and inner sides so that the meaning is only fully understood when it has been entered and looked back on:

A COTTAGE • A FIELD • A PLOUGH

outside, and on the garden side:

THERE IS HAPPINESS

– words borrowed from the most morally uncompromising of the French Revolutionary leaders, Louis Antoine Saint-Just, whose detestation of weak and bad citizenship was as strong as his love of the simple, co-operative way of life of the French country people. Consider here one of Finlay's Detached Sentences:

Certain gardens are described as retreats when they are really attacks.

The paradox – the unexpected challenge to assumptions and the revelation of depth in the apparently simple – will be a recurring feature of the garden.

Deep in the Wild Garden, where the path leads on to the upper ponds, stand two imposing gate piers crowned by what seem, at a casual glance, to be classical urns or finials, but are hand grenades of the British Second World War design, often nicknamed 'pineapples' because of their shape. They stand monumentally made from stone, their firing rings draping over their shoulders as ivy might over the expected finials; a characteristic conundrum whose elements are humour, beauty and threat.

A very different little wicket gate is set into the fence surrounding the Stonypath Allotment. Its simple inscription *KAILYARD* repeats the name given to the late-nineteenth-century group of Scottish writers such as J.M. Barrie and S.R. Crockett who treated the lives and concerns of Scots people in a sentimental way often unjustly scorned by critics. Kail, sometimes spelled kale, a particularly hardy kind of cabbage, was at one time a staple of the Scottish diet and its usurpation in contemporary life

by more glamorously exotic foods is not likely to have done the Scots much good.

In an upland garden such as this it is appropriate to find stiles connecting the wilder hillsides with the tamer garden, and there are two connecting the upper pond garden with the moorland. A philosophical one has a triple

inscription in the manner of Friedrich Hegel, whose idealism held reason to be the heart of reality. The proposition reads *THESIS fence ANTITHESIS gate,* then, as the farther side is reached, *SYNTHESIS stile.*

The adapted dictionary definition, a device Finlay uses frequently, underlines the poetic and literary nature of his

work. The apparent precision and conciseness of a definition is brought to bear in ways which reveal unexpected aspects of the objects they describe and often dissolve the accepted meaning of terms, or interpretation of their reference in the 'real' world. The second stile carries such a definition of its physical and its ideal nature:

STILE n. an escalation of the footpath

Water is almost omnipresent in the garden, with ponds, lochan and streams plentifully fed by the rain falling on the hillside. An imposing aqueduct brings a trickle of water to splash down and continue as a stream just beside a tablet inscribed with lines from Homer's *Iliad*, Book IV, in Greek and Alexander Pope's English translation:

> *Workd into sudden rage by wintry showrs*
> *Down the steep hill the roaring torrent pours*
> *The mountain shepherd hears the distant noise*

The stream flows on through the Middle Pond beneath an arch of stone inscribed *WAVE*. The word *wave*, the tide of the stream, is made to contain the Latin *ave*, the formal word of greeting. Thus an attitude of reverence is suggested to the human observer as the stream greets in homage the spirit of the pool as it passes through.

The sounds of the rush, splash and trickle of the streams and fountains are as much part of the garden as the sheen and flicker of the rills and ponds. Bridges and stepping stones lead the way from bank to bank. Spanning the stream between the Wild Garden and Lochan Eck, as the gaze travels towards the receding moors, there is a bridge of pink concrete, a single word cut into its side – *CLAUDI* – the signature of Claude Lorrain. So the vista of classical ruin, rippling water, sussurating grasses and rustling trees beyond the bridge is transfigured into a landscape as he might have painted it, a reinvention of nature after art, with an element of grandeur added by the huge stands of rhubarb ('the poor man's gunnera', IHF) growing beside the bridge.

On a stepping stone in the Middle Pond, taking the footsteps only an easy distance from the grassy verge and into the other element, another definition dissolves the boundaries and restrictions we place on perception:

RIPPLE n. A FOLD. A FLUTING OF
THE LIQUID ELEMENT

The flow of the elegantly carved Roman letters over the uneven surface of the wild stone intensifies the effect.

In the English Parkland three more bridges invite consideration of concepts and images by means of their material construction and their inscriptions. Incised on a simple plank across the stream which has come skidding down over the sluice from Lochan Eck are words describing the appearance of the water beneath. The shapes of the foam on the water fallen from the sluice are variations on a theme which the unelaborated words offer for our delight:

RCHER AN ARCHITECTURAL TERM A MATERIAL CURVE SUSTAINED BY GRAVITY AS RAPTURE BY GRIEF

lines of Foam strings of Foam strands of Foam ropes of Foam lacings of Foam

lines of foam
strings of foam
strands of foam
ropes of foam
lacings of foam

An arched stone bridge illuminates beautifully the relation of suffering and joy as it simply describes itself.

Pages 34–35 The stream with its lade skirts the English Parkland.

ARCH n. AN ARCHITECTURAL TERM
A MATERIAL CURVE SUSTAINED BY GRAVITY
AS RAPTURE BY GRIEF

Two wooden planks set over the stream echo a paradoxical proposition of the pre-Socratic philosopher Heraclitus. The simplicity of the statement belies the complexity of its implications:

THAT WHICH JOINS AND THAT WHICH
DIVIDES IS ONE AND THE SAME

The stream's course inspired a further series of works. It runs past three plinths set in the water, their inscriptions reading:

STONY	FRECKLED	PEBBLED
STREAM	FRESHET	BROOK

to a slender wooden channel with a slate tablet inscribed:

LINE. LIGHT. LADE.

bringing together the drawn line as the essence of art, the thin gleam of the water in its wooden confines, and the shifting associations of the word 'lade' – a ship's cargo, ladles, loading with bounty, leading water to a mill race. Next, it passes a bench inviting a pause to meditate on its words:

OAK BARK BOAT

the tree linked to the boat it might become by the ambiguity of 'bark' – the old literary word. After that, three more plinths set in the water develop the same theme:

LEAF & BOAT   BOAT & BARK   BARK & LEAF

The spring feeding the Temple Pool splashes from a stone shell recalling Botticelli's *The Birth of Venus*. Carved in it is:

CADDIS SHELL   GODDESS SHELL

The abandoned 'shell' of the caddis fly larva, made from little stones and pieces of plant stems, is easily found in Scottish burns and pools. The elegant shell of Venus, goddess of love

born from the sea, can only be found in myth and art. Both evoke idylls to remember and cherish.

Beside the path on the hillside of the Wild Garden are two sobering works. The first is a memorial stone to *MAN A PASSERBY*, while the second is a low bench inscribed with the words:

NOTHINGNESS NIHILATING AS TIME IN SPACE
IS WHAT MAKES MAN A PASSERBY
IN THE SPATIAL WORLD. KOJÈVE

Our transitory state is first marked with sad simplicity, then with more challenging explication quoted from Alexandre Kojève's book on the work of the philosopher Hegel.

THE SEA

Attached to a tree on the boundary of Little Sparta a stone plaque reads:

MARE
NOSTRUM

Our Sea – the name given by the Romans to the Mediterranean, the sea their empire enclosed and dominated. Fitted round the base of the tree is a wooden bench with the inscription:

THE SEA'S WAVES
THE WAVES' SHEAVES
THE SEA'S NAVES

The two inscriptions invite us to recognize Little Sparta as a domain, that is a realm of particular character, ideals and power, while they alert the ear to the sounds and the eye to the sights of this inland garden. The Latin of the first inscription signals the moral aspect of the domain – here the principles of artistic truth and order will be paramount and actively defended when necessary; the cadence of the words on the bench reflects the swell and sound of the sea. The rushing and rustling of the wind in the branches, the bending and tossing of the grasses and reeds on the surrounding moorland have their parallel in the sound and sight of the sea; and on stormy days the garden with its

artfully constructed plantings and installations is buffeted by great gusts as if it were a boat battling through the onslaught of a wind-driven tide. The meaning of the words, allied to their sound, conjures up in imagination the movement of water and of harvested corn, then the unexpected *Naves* takes us to another level by visualizing the valley between rolling waves as a church's nave, the central aisle leading to the altar, so that the sea becomes a sacred space to be entered with reverence. A final layer of meaning comes with the derivation of the word 'nave' from the Latin *navis*, a ship.

For all of us the sea is a haunting symbol. It is the element from which life emerges, it is Isaac Newton's 'vast ocean of truth', it is the undiscoverable, inevitable prospect gazed upon in Caspar David Friedrich's paintings, not to be explained, but only acknowledged. Throughout the garden there are works which depend on the idea of the sea as a context or as a universal idea from which metaphors may be trawled. Some of the ideas and meanings which are at the heart of the works are full of tranquillity, some are challenging in the violent tragedies they employ.

On the clipped grass lawn of the English Parkland a landwork, slightly puzzling from a distance, makes land and sea congruent; the smooth surface of the lawn has been moulded into a series of five little hillocks on each of which a roughly dressed stone block is set. Coming closer

to the work one sees that cut into each block is the word for wave, each in a different language:

WAVE VAGUE WOGE ONDA UNDA

The undulating land has become the sea; the stones, fragments, as it were, from a terrestrial monument, have become vessels floating on the crests of the waves. There is a carefully constructed variety in the sound and appearance of their single word. As the vowel sounds change progressively through the five words, so also the initial consonants of the first three give way to the softer, central consonants of the last two, as the progress of a wave moves from its building up to its resolution.

In front of the house there is a wide pathway, almost a terrace, separating the house from the Front Garden's fringe of sweet cicely. Potted plants, a water butt and a wooden bench share the space with many small works of art. Among them are three works using only five words between them but with much imagery and meaning compressed into them. *Unda* – the Latin word for wave – is picked out in mosaic letters alternating with the proof-reading sign for the transposition of letters, a shape like the curl of a breaking wave, all in shades of blue. In this context of the proof-reader's switching of typographical elements, the shapes and words of the mosaic evoke the constantly changing rise and fall of the water's surface, switched into

the earth element of the concrete surrounding it. Two further works using mosaic are near by.

WAVE
SHEAF

brings together two words charged with associations of sea and land, the first in blue letters, the second in yellow. Imagining a cornfield of times past with the sheaves propped up together in long rows, their plumy heads curling and moving in the breeze, we can see the long breakers coming into shore, their crests foaming and turning.

SEA
PINK

instantly brings to mind the pale, hardy little flowers adorning every tussocky, windblown seaside. The saturated colours of the mosaic and its background also call up another image, that of the hot Mediterranean pinks and blues used for example by Matisse in paintings of Provence. Another graphic touch is added by the word pink's less well known meaning as a small sea-going vessel. As so often with Finlay's work, affectionate memories are

brought together to enhance each other and generate a celebration of the manifold beauty of the world as it is and as it is shown to us by art.

Another work whose brief simplicity contains endless possibilities for the imagination is a small stone block in the Woodland Garden with a carved inscription:

A ⌇ O R

The wave-shaped proof-reading sign here brings to mind the motion of a boat as the rower's body bends, the oar dips and the boat surges forward, rising and falling through the waves, which sometimes make its shape indistinct. It is left to the viewer of the work to consider which sea, real or mythical, the oar is cutting through, and pulled by whom. Near this work there is a wooden pole with the inscription:

BLUE • WATER'S • BARK

Again the imagination is invited to see beyond the words to a ship, a tree and water, salt or fresh. A blue-painted ship, the bark of a tree that became a ship, the blue shadows in a wood, the blue sea, the sky reflected in a woodland pool.

On an elegaic stone tablet erected beside the Temple Pool in the manner of a memorial stone beside a grave the carved inscription reads:

HIC IACET
PARVULUM
QUODDAM
EX AQUA
LONGIORE
EXCERPTUM

'Here lies a small excerpt from a longer water' – should we smile or cry? 'Here lies' – always a marker of death, and how poignant to think of the Pool as *parvulum quoddam* – a tiny little thing – cut out from the great Ocean and placed here to be visited in its resting place. 'From a longer water' – but since we would expect the sentence to end with a longer 'work', a work of literature, we can find an implicit invitation to 'read' the Pool and give attention to its fish, frogs, weeds and ripples.

A more serious but equally tender pair of epitaphs is inscribed on a slate bird bath in the Front Garden, surrounded by a tangle of foliage and flowers. They commemorate a ship destroyed in the First World War, the first lamenting the fate of the ship, the second addressing the sea, pleading for the schooner's safekeeping:

EPITAPH
the Little Secret
schooner (torpedoed 1917)

Here, a tin-fish in her hold,
Lies the Little Secret, *told.*
or
Ocean, keep this Secret *well*
Safe from shot and shell & shell.

The tragedy of the lost ship is the more affecting because of its half-playful, intimate name, the *Little Secret*, betrayed

and now carrying within it the agent of its destruction, a 'tin-fish', the slang name given to early torpedoes which veils the real nature of the weapon. The personified Ocean becomes a saviour and comforter, trusted not to 'tell' the Secret, and to protect the *Little Secret* from the ravages of both sea bed and war.

Two works which link the land and the sea in very different ways are to be found, one in the Allotment and one in the English Parkland. Walking from the front of the house towards the Allotment the visitor is guided by a wooden signpost with one direction on its arm: *DIEPPE*. Turning the corner one sees the destination – two wooden sheds in line together, one for storing tools and garden equipment, the other for the gardener to keep his boots in, with an extra jersey perhaps, and a comfortable, battered chair beside his radio where he eats his lunch and keeps his thermos handy. Such landlocked functions are swept away by the trope of the sheds as beach huts facing not the windy moorland of Lanarkshire but the sea breezes of the French side of the Channel, with bathers inside changing into swimming dress of whatever period the imagination chooses – perhaps Impressionist bathers; possibly men in striped bathing suits and straw hats; and mussels for lunch later on?

The other work consists of three white-painted wooden beehives set in a line together under the shade of

some trees. Each bears a blue-painted title on the front, the name and port registration letters and numbers of a Scottish fishing boat. Finlay's wide knowledge of boats and ships and their accoutrements is an endless source of imagery which he uses in his work in the way a composer may embed folk tunes in a symphony. So here the boat names and numbers

BOUNTIFUL UL 238
SWEET PROMISE FH 172
GOLDEN GAIN FR 59

are attached to the beehives. Honey, the fruit of the bees' harvesting from the hillside flowers, would normally be in the hives, but here they are linked to the harvest from the sea made by fishing boats like the ones whose names and port letters they bear. The names are reminiscent of land harvests gathered in a peaceful and benign autumn. The images of the bees and their sweet golden honey, the men in their little boats sailing home to Ullapool, Falmouth or Fraserburgh, the holds filled with fish, along with the pastoral idyll inherent in the boat names, assume a symbolic power to celebrate the brave beauty of toil for sustenance.

Gardens are made more charming by their furnishings – benches, trellises, arbours and sundials. Two of Little Sparta's sundials make use of boat names to illustrate the passing of the seasons as a frame to the passing of the hours. A white marble table has the dial and inscription on its surface:

THE FOUR SEASONS IN SAIL
Spring – Clipper
Summer – Mumble Bee
Autumn – Wood Barque
Winter – Wood Snow

As the seasons sail by, these trading schooners let us visualize the attributes of each, calling up our own memories and associations. Snipping and pruning in the fresh, still chilly brightness of springtime; the heavy, bumbling flight of a soporifically humming bee in a summer meadow; the low

evening sunlight of autumn catching the relief patterns of tree bark tangling with the image of a barque – Arthurian or from a scene by Watteau? – drifting off into the sunset; winter snow drifting over the cold, still wood.

Fixed on the old stone wall of the Temple building a ceramic sundial presents the seasons as fore-and-afters, two-masted ships, ketch-rigged to make them better equipped to face foul or fair weather:

THE FOUR SEASONS AS FORE-AND-AFTERS
      the Kathleen & May   *the Minnie Flossie*
      the Samuel Moss   *the William Ashburner*

Each of the boat names, all of them real, is filled with hints of the seasons' special attributes. May blossom, white and foamy, and the promise of a pretty girl; the gleam of flowers and the countrified pet names; the soft dampness of autumnal moss and the tougher note of masculinity; the cold, the ashes of the year, the glow of fires.

Two more boat names appear on a sundial of weathered wood in the Front Garden, with a thread of anxiety for the safety of the boat and the propitiousness of the weather running through the image of lavish harvest, whether of fish or fruit:

BE IN TIME   FRUITFUL VINE

Another sundial makes use of more abstract and philosophical imagery in conjunction with the language of commerce, the human element. The words are few and simple:

AZURE & SON
ISLANDS LTD
OCEANS INC

but the ideas contained in them have large connotations. Azure is the pure blue of the cloudless sky, the symbol of infinity, the domain of Zeus, the locus of Christian Heaven and the element of pre-Socratic ether. The meaning of Son hovers between the Son of the Trinity or Apollo, the son of Zeus and, to the ear, Sun, as both Apollo's attribute and the condensation of the ether into fire. Islands represent the most dense condensation of matter, limited by their

nature and defined by the oceans flowing round them and making the tally of the four elements complete. Finlay's light touch succeeds in bringing a complex of universal concepts together in the clipped format of business nomenclature, with no suggestion of taint or disparagement, indeed with the implication of system and good order.

H)OUR LADY

is the text on a small stone sundial in the Wild Garden. The simply sketched figure of the Madonna holds out her cloak, inscribed with the hour lines, to shelter repentant sinners. Her cloak, traditionally of blue, identifies her as a merciful presence encompassing the sheltering sky above us. Across the pond from this work is another small sundial of weathered wood. It faces west, so only tells the evening hours. The relief carving shows a little sail and the words:

EVENING WILL COME
THEY WILL SEW THE BLUE SAIL

The end of the day, the end of life, the repairing of the day's damage to fishermen's sails, the preparation for infinity.

Up on the moor a slender stone column standing fully in the sun has a definition carved on it:

SHADOW n. THE HOUR HAND

Moving slowly.

At the bottom of the Front Garden, set before a hedge of thorn bushes, a stone bench invites the visitor to stop and rest. The inscription on it reads:

A SPRAY FROM A
BRETON SEA-HEDGE
THONIER

Once again land and sea are merged in a metaphor whose decipherment brings pleasure at its delicacy and perfection. A thonier – the word overlaps visually and aurally with the English thorn – is a French tuna fishing boat sailing from a Breton port far out into the Atlantic with its characteristic gear of two long rods fitted with hooks on either side of the mast. The sea-hedge is the boat with its spray of thorny rods poised to catch the tuna as the Stonypath hedge may catch the unwary visitor's sleeve, or imagination.

Not far from the bench a wooden pole catches the eye, a stripped sapling painted white, with an incised poem:

roses   roses

roses   rove

roses   reefed

The purity of the white wood with its knots showing through matches the simple beauty of the roses, which are conceived as rambling, or roving, their little flowers perhaps starring the plant and its support as the letter *r* does the poem. The second image is of the ropes threaded through eyelets and finally knotting up a sail. Rove and reefed are different tenses of the nautical term for this, familiar to sailors whether of great yachts or tiny patched-up dinghies.

A little further on another stone bench has an inscription inviting the imagination to discover Finlay's affectionate metaphor:

AN ORCHARD

OF RUSSETS

APPLEDORE

The charmingly named Devon port of Appledore, in a county famous for its apple orchards, was well known for its harbour, regularly crowded with sailing ships and boats,

most of them with sails of russet-brown. Once again ideas of harvests and their provenance are blended and simply offered in a way that asks the reader of the bench to visualize, explore, and enjoy in imagination.

A feeling of great sadness lies hidden in the text of a sundial set in the water at the edge of the Temple Pool. The *titulus* round its face reads

TRISTRAM'S SAIL WIND SHADOW

It surrounds text taken from a sailing handbook:

The shadow has an axis which is the apparent wind direction. Outwardly from the boat it cannot extend for an infinite distance and its area becomes narrower the further away from the boat one moves. The effect is said to be felt up to seven mast lengths away.

Despite the love between Tristram and the princess Isolde, out of duty she married his uncle, King Mark, and Tristram sailed away from Cornwall to marry Iseult of the white hand. Wounded in battle, he knew that only Isolde could heal him and he sent a message asking her to come to him and to have a white sail hoisted on her ship to show she was on board. When jealous Iseult saw the white sail approaching she falsely told Tristram it was black, and in despair he died.

The wind shadow is the effect felt when one boat cuts in between another and the wind, so that the second boat loses its momentum. The metaphor implicitly drawn out on the sundial is of the love and sorrow brought upon the characters of the legend. The poignancy is the more affecting through the juxtaposition of the tragedy and the prosaic language of the sailing handbook.

TRISTRAM'S SAIL · MOVING SHADOW · WIND ·

The shadow
has an axis which is
the apparent wind direction.
Outwardly from the boat it cannot
extend for an infinite distance and its
area becomes narrower the further away
from the boat one moves. The effect is said
to be felt up to seven mast lengths away.

HYPERBOREAN

APOLLO

A preoccupation with the need to make works embodying ideals of purity, alongside the conviction that evil and good are forces to be perceived and acted upon with resolute integrity, drew Finlay to the philosophy, religion and poetry of Greece and Rome. The richness of the classical tradition and its pervasion of Western culture are reaffirmed and made freshly striking throughout the garden.

The pre-Socratic philosophers' use of paradox and metaphor in their cosmologies, made all the more gnomic now by being so fragmentary, becomes the source of a poetically potent vocabulary of words and images used to illumine contemporary versions of theology and ethics. The works of the Roman poets Virgil and Ovid, both writing at the dawning of the Empire, have been treasures drawn on by Western artists throughout the subsequent two millennia, and Finlay has added to this store. Writing from political patriotism and love of the Italian countryside, Virgil embodies magisterial command of language and purpose with tender affection and an underlying melancholic loneliness. Ovid's predilection for wit, love and loveliness suffuses his works and colours particularly his collection of

seminal myths, the *Metamorphoses*. Finlay's mastery of metaphor and icon drew him to explore these Changes.

At the heart of Little Sparta stands the garden temple, more centrally situated than most such neoclassical and romantic temples of the eighteenth and early nineteenth centuries, and more complex since it is not simply decorative. It is dedicated to Apollo, his Music, his Missiles, his Muses. The beautiful god Apollo was the upholder of civilization in its destructive and positive elements. It was he who delivered prophetic answers through his priestess Pythia to a questioning world, and he who dealt in terror and death as the far-shooting archer. He was the guardian of healing powers and of the rule of law. God of music, with the Muses he presided over all the arts and throughout the countryside he was the protector of flocks and herds. A lesser but charming role was as the killer of mice in farm and cottage. The Little Sparta Temple of Apollo, before its transformation on this return of the god to his northern, Hyperborean domain, was one of the old farm buildings, a stone-built byre. As Finlay declares in a much later work, 'Art is a small adjustment', and this temple to the god of art (as well as farm beasts) retains its unassuming Scottish rural character, with Corinthian and Ionic columns not actually built but simply painted on the façades, to suggest a classical temple porch, and fluted elements added at the door and windows. Painted also are the words of dedication:

TO APOLLO
HIS MUSIC   HIS MISSILES   HIS MUSES

The reader is prompted to consider the meaning of words and ideas from one culture being transposed into another. Apollo's instrument was the lyre, the instrument of lyrical song and poem, the vehicle for heartfelt celebration. His missiles were his deadly arrows, fast, accurate and elegant as

Left and above right Two sets of ceramic pipes of Pan. On one Pythagoras's understanding of the Universe as harmony is linked to the music of Pan. The words on the other are *VIRTUE IS HARMONY*.

a stealth bomber or a laser-guided rocket. His Muses were the goddesses who gave inspiration to the most elevated of the arts, and we may have to reassess our ideas of what constitutes an elevated art in our time, and what inspires it.

Since the Little Spartan War the interior of the temple has not been permitted to fulfil its intended function as a sacred space for the display of art works; but facing it across the Temple Pool is another smaller temple, this one dedicated to Baucis and Philemon. Ovid's moving account of their story inspired its creation and embellishment. The gods Zeus and Hermes travelling together through the Phrygian countryside were overtaken by nightfall and came disguised as mortals to the humble cottage of the old man Philemon and his wife, Baucis, to ask for shelter. The old couple welcomed the unrecognized gods into their simple home and gave them what food they had. Acknowledging their goodness, Zeus transformed their little house into a beautiful temple and appointed the two old people to be its priests. On their death they were transformed into trees standing before their door. Their temple at Little Sparta represents the moment of its

transformation, with a premonition of the old couple's final form. The unadorned, low farm building has a porch of two undressed tree trunks supporting a stone architrave, one half of which is still rough, while the other is polished smooth. The roof is of slates, but the first few of them are gilded as the miraculous change takes place. The temple's interior, not now a single bare room for storing fodder or farm equipment, is furnished with a long table and chairs,

the echo of the peasants' hospitality, an altar, stone texts upon the walls and statues by the door. Simple piety and human kindness are endowed with dignity.

Close by, another shrine of classical design is set against a wall and shaded by little trees. It is a Roman lararium, a shrine dedicated to the patron god of a household, and between its columns the statue, based on a work by the Italian Baroque sculptor Gian Lorenzo Bernini, shows a lithe young god clad only in a flowing length of cloth and running forward eagerly, a machine gun in his hand. The inscribed letters on his plinth *A SJ* tell us that he is Apollo as Saint-Just. Three icons brought together to jar one's mind and feelings. The attributes of Apollo are transmitted

to the young French Revolutionary, whose missiles were those of his unflinching attacks on failure to achieve a pure revolution, and the physical weapon in his hand is the contemporary warrior's quick-firing instrument of destruction. The bringing together of the ideals of integrity and truth with violence requires a judgement about the role of violent action in our or any world view.

The same idea lies behind a spectacular work beside the Upper Pond. A gigantic gilded head emerges from the rough grass, as if a huge cult statue had fallen here long ago and left only the head still visible. It is a classical head of Apollo with two words incised on the brow – *APOLLON TERRORISTE*. The use of French directs us again to the

implacable Saint-Just, architect of the Terror, and the comparison is drawn with Apollo's treatment of the satyr Marsyas, defeated by him in an ill-advised musical contest when Marsyas tried to outdo him by playing on the flute of Athene. Tied to a tree and flayed alive, 'Why do you tear me from myself?' he says in Ovid's account of the agony. 'Ah, I am sorry, ah, the flute is not worth so much.' But die he does, without the silent dignity shown by Saint-Just when his time came at the guillotine.

Ovid's story of Apollo and Daphne is a familiar one – the young god is suddenly and for the first time in love with the nymph Daphne, who as suddenly hates the thought of love, for both have been struck by angry Cupid's arrows, one of which kindles love and one which brings aversion. Apollo pursues her as she flees through the woods, until in her despair she calls on her father, the river god Peneus, to save her. At once she becomes numb and stiffens as she is changed into a laurel tree, keeping of her beauty only the gleam of evergreen leaves. Apollo, distraught, vows that laurel leaves shall always constitute the garlands for his brow, his lyre and his quiver. In the garden the two figures are designed after the marble group by Bernini, but they are cut from sheet metal and enamelled, he a burning red and she the green that presages her fate. There are multiple layers of association and meaning to ponder here. Ovid's story dwells on the violent nature of love, its unjust power and its perplexing or tragic results. But Daphne's metamorphosis is brought about by her loving father, as she implores him, and Apollo's love is made unending and pure by his adoption of her leaves as his symbol. Bernini's group freezes the passionate chase in marble, the classically perfect medium, while Finlay's makes the pair at once flagrant by their colours and fugitive in their almost two-dimensionality.

Two works in the Front Garden focus on the godling Hypnos, the god of sleep. The fatherless child of Night, he is portrayed in a classical head found near Perugia as a young

man with wings sprouting from his temples; his disturbing Little Spartan herm, made from black resin and mounted on a column beside dark fir trees, has wings sprouting from his eyes. Further up the garden he appears again, celebrated with his brother Thanatos, Death, on two stones inscribed:

HYPNOS	*THANATOS*
HIS WINGS	*OUR STONES*
TROUBLE	*SUMMON*
HIS EYES	*YOUR MOSS*

As in another idiom children's eyes are troubled by sand sprinkled by the Sandman to help them fall asleep, the wings of Hypnos bring on his sleep. The moss-covered stone of Thanatos evokes at once a mossy gravestone and an Ozymandian concept of human achievements sinking into the kind obscurity of decay.

Throughout the garden there are fragments of classical 'ruins', half-buried sections of architrave, toppled columns and capitals. The view down the Front Garden is punctuated by three such classical references. A spirally fluted column, a column in the neoclassical manner of the eighteenth-century French architect Claude-Nicolas Ledoux, with cubes inserted into it, and an intriguing fragment of statuary. This is one of Finlay's visual jokes. It is a piece of coloured concrete set over a sheet of corrugated iron to produce a fluted effect. Placed aslant on its plinth it is masquerading as a fragment of billowing drapery on a classical statue, perhaps a Winged Victory!

Up in the Wild Garden a little pool in the downward flow of the stream that runs through the garden is dedicated to the goddess Artemis in her Greek guise or Diana as a Roman. It recalls the pool where the hunter Actaeon inadvertently saw her bathing. In angry revenge she changed him into a stag and he was torn to pieces by his own dogs. The arch through which the water from the pool flows onwards is inscribed with two felicitously

discovered fishing boat names with their port letters and numbers, on one side *ARTEMIS FR 15* from Fraserburgh, and on the other *DIANA SY 86* from Stornoway.

Close to Lochan Eck, just as the land rises away from the clipped grass of the pathways, there is a group comprising column and plinth with scattered stone blocks, one of which bears the inscription:

THE WORLD HAS BEEN EMPTY
SINCE THE ROMANS
SAINT-JUST

Again the parallel is drawn between Saint-Just and the idealized achievement of Republican Rome, whose fall left the world bereft of the moral strength that is prepared to fight, kill and die for a principle.

In the hillside across the path a gate of iron railings guards a grotto with a façade of undressed stone and a smooth keystone engraved with *A* and *D*, a lightning flash between them. Inside the grotto an oculus in the roof gives enough light to see two niches each with a bust, one of Dido and one of Aeneas. A frieze runs round the wall with lettering:

ONE CAVE A GRATEFUL SHELTER SHALL AFFORD TO THE FAIR PRINCESS AND THE TROJAN LORD.

Aeneas, prince of Troy, fled from his defeated city and sailed west to find the promised land where he was destined to found a new city which one day would become Rome. He was shipwrecked on the coast of Africa, at the city of Carthage, and was welcomed by its Queen, Dido, who fell in love with him. One fateful day when they were out hunting a storm blew up; they found shelter in a cave alone together and made love as the lightning flashes signalled disaster. In the aftermath of this encounter Aeneas was reminded of his destiny, and in sorrow sailed away to find his fated land, leaving Dido to kill herself and knowing nothing of the eventual destruction of Carthage by Rome. In Dryden's translation of Virgil's lines quoted on the frieze of the grotto, Finlay not only recalls and celebrates the story of love and loss but gives an idealized setting or illustration of the critical moment emphasized by the two busts.

Rather as a living tree trunk in another context might have names cut into it, perhaps with a heart pierced by an arrow, so a ruined block by the side of the lochan bears a roughly carved inscription:

AENEAS ET DIDO

Taking the motif of Dido into another theatre of tragedy, a polished stone column records a list of cruisers of the Dido class sunk during the Second World War.

TRAGEDIES
of the
DIDO
class cruisers
1941–1944
Bonaventure torpd. Mar 41
Naiad torpd. Mar 42
Hermione torpd. June 42
Charybdis torpd. Oct 43
Spartan bombd. Jan 44
TENDEBANTQUE MANUS RIPAE ULTERIORIS
AMORE

The sadly ironic placing of Bonaventure first in this list of doomed ships, all the others classically named, emphasizes the high hopes and the lost lives of the sinkings. The Latin words for 'And they were stretching out their hands in longing for the farther bank' are from the sixth book of Virgil's *Aeneid*, describing the souls of the unburied dead, such as the men of the cruisers, who cannot peacefully go to their sad home in the Underworld but must wait displaced for long years on the bank of the dividing River Styx, until the ferryman Charon is at last permitted to take them across.

Finlay uses the Latin language to cast a certain dignity and deliberate obscurity over the meaning of works, as a funerary urn beneath the shade of some birch trees enunciates:

COGITATIO
SUB UMBRA
LATINAE
CELATA

'A thought hidden beneath the shade of Latin.' Finlay's work constantly makes use of the spareness of the Latin language, which is well suited to the expression of compressed or gnomic meaning. Thus *cogitatio* may be a thought, or perhaps meditation. The urn suggests the death of Latin as the *lingua franca* of Europe, and its setting in the shade of a tree is more resonant because of the secondary meaning of *umbra* – a ghost. Overall the work points to a central theme in the garden, that the past and its material or cultural relics are essential exemplars for the present.

This eclecticism is made very clear in a glade near by where a large Corinthian capital, bereft of its column, is placed beside a wooden bench around the base of a beech tree. It bears the words *ELECTIS ARBORIBUS AMOENISSIMUS* – 'Most delightful with its chosen trees'. Describing a holy mountainside where ancient astrologers watched for the star which led the Magi to Bethlehem, this is a quotation from the *Patrologia Latina*, a collection of the works of Early Church Fathers made by the nineteenth-century priest Jacques-Paul Migne.

Virgil's Spring marks the entry into Little Sparta of the stream which feeds all the ponds. The words come from Virgil's tenth *Eclogue* and we may read them as describing the spiritual pleasures of art as well as the delightful physical aspects of the garden.

HIC   *HIC*

GELIDI FONTES   *MOLLIA PRATA*

Here are cool springs   *here soft meadows*

VIRGIL ECLOGUES

Two slate plaques describe their setting and evoke its visual and aural aspects by transposing the adjectives. Once again English is used to describe Nature and Latin Art:

THE	*LUCUS*
SHADY	*UMBROSUS*
GROVE	
THE	*RIVUS*
MURMURING	*MURMURANS*
STREAM	
THE	*RIVUS*
SHADY	*UMBROSUS*
STREAM	
THE	*LUCUS*
MURMURING	*MURMURANS*
GROVE	

On the brick floor of the Woodland Garden, concrete blocks cast on corrugated iron are arranged to signify tank tracks, a symbol of the warfare that has at times engulfed Little Sparta.

CONFLICT

Systems of philosophy from the pre-Socratic to the neo-Platonist have discussed the ideas of conflict and interaction in the widest of senses. In the sixth century BC Anaximander introduced the concept of four elements in opposition to each other as the basis of the universe – water, earth, air and fire; Heraclitus proposed that things were defined and given existence by their opposites, so light and darkness are opposite aspects of the same thing. The essential conflict between nature and art, chaos and order, wildness and civilization sums up much of the principle of Little Sparta as an art work. The acceptance of conflict and the concomitant necessity to perceive what is right and pure brings us face to face with sometimes uncomfortable truths and dilemmas which Finlay identifies and resolves in his use of images which are didactic as well as beautiful. The fifth-century neo-Platonist teacher Proclus, in his Commentary on Plato's *Alcibiades I,* says: 'Now we observe that physical beauty exists only when form prevails over matter: for matter is ugly and devoid of beauty, and form when overpowered by it is filled with ugliness and shapelessness and becomes as it were formless, being assimilated to the underlying nature.' This most fundamental exposition is illustrated by a large pink fibreglass cube, a perfect geometric form which has had a corner, as it were, dismantled or not completed, to

show the underlying rough and unharmonious internal matter which has been utterly changed by the imposition of the cube form which organizes matter and brings into being a new entity that is comprehensible aesthetically and intellectually.

Roman Stoics, taking the hero Hercules as an exemplar of physical and mental strength, believed that courageous participation in the good government of state or individual was a mark of the good man, and that such courageous virtue was pre-eminently developed and demonstrated by embracing the conflict of just warfare. The Second World War and subsequent developments in armaments have proved to be a fertile source of imagery in Finlay's exploration of the nature of conflict.

One of the most enigmatic works in the garden is a simplified stone aircraft carrier which, by its shape initially, suggests an altar. Its only inscription, taking on the role of an altar's *titulus*, reads *II 1019*. This is the reference number for an entry in the *Stoicorum Veterum Fragmenta*, a collection of the fragmentary writings of the Stoic philosophers of classical times. The words of Chrysippus translated read: 'Gods may be known to exist on account of their altars.' Here Finlay's work, like so many in the garden, deliberately conceals its meaning, requiring us to uncover its true essence, to think, and allow the layers of meaning slowly to become clear. Classical altars were dedicated to particular gods; Christian altars to God in some form, or to a saint. This work prompts us to ask what is our god now, and what his altar? One answer is Power, with its attributes of destruction and glory, and its altar here is its instrument, the aircraft carrier. In the ancient world altars received offerings which were to be burnt; in this work we can extrapolate from the carrier to its aircraft, engulfed in the fires of their own exploded fuel or the fire power of the enemy. Ancient offerings were sacrifices, given from fear or self-interest, or from noble piety. Whatever the god, the ideas of sacrifice and piety elicit from us a commensurate response.

A round slate plaque mounted on a brick plinth bears an inscription whose letters are spaced so as to echo the satisfyingly complete circular form, but with a separate central line identifying event, time and place, the Pacific battle of Midway, fought on 4 June 1942. Above this line the words are in Latin, below in English.

HIC
PERIERVNT AKAGI
KAGA SORYV HIRYV YORK-
TOWN AEQVORIS ALVI MEL SVVM
FLAMMIFERVM EA CONSVMPSIT
VNACVM EXAMINIBVS OPTIMIS

BATTLE OF MIDWAY 4 JUNE 1942

HERE PERISHED AKAGI KAGA SORYU
HIRYU YORKTOWN THE SEA-HIVES
CONSUMED WITH THEIR MOST
CHOICE SWARMS BY THEIR
OWN FLAME-BEARING
HONEY

This battle, fought around a tiny island, was the turning point of the war in the Pacific. The Japanese attempts to reach Hawaii were thwarted and the aircraft carrier was

HIC
PERIERVNT AKAGI
KAGA SORYV HIRYV YORK
TOWII ÆQVORIS ALVI MEL SVVI
FLAMMIFERVM EA CONSVMPSIT
VNACVM EXAMINIBVS OPTIMIS

BATTLE OF MIDWAY 4 JUNE 1942

HERE PERISHED AKAGI KAGA SORYV
HIRYV YORKTOWN THE SEA-HIVES
CONSUMED WITH THEIR MOST
CHOICE SWARMS BY THEIR
OWN FLAME-BEARING
HONEY

established as the pre-eminently successful instrument of warfare at sea. However, it is the tragedy and pathos of the battle in which both American and Japanese aircraft carriers and planes were destroyed that Finlay celebrates, endowing it with heroic dignity by using the perfect circle of dark slate and the Latin words and letters, and deepening both heroism and poignancy by the startling imagery of bees, hives and honey, which adds a Virgilian gloss to the elegy, recalling his description in the last book of the *Aeneid* where a shepherd smokes out a bees' nest and their loud humming rises with the billowing smoke of their destruction.

In a different part of the garden another work commemorates the same battle and throws a sombre gleam of light on the implications of that day's meaning to us all. It is a stone inscribed with five resonant words:

THROUGH A DARK WOOD
MIDWAY

an echo of Dante as, at the beginning of the *Divine Comedy*, he describes a despairing inner struggle – 'In the middle of the journey of our life I found myself in a dark wood.'

The sea and ships are brought together with bees, beehives and leafy glades, in another work which meditates on the conflicting ideas of war and peace, earth and water. A semi-abstract hive, reminiscent of a gravestone, bears the words:

HIVES THRU LEAVES
WINGS THRU WAVES

The sound and the appearance of 'leaves' and 'waves' conjures up the sea; 'thru' not 'through' indicates America; 'hives' and 'wings' bring out the central idea of the poem. We are to think of a mid-Pacific battle of the Second World War, between America and Japan. What we see in the first line is what is before our eyes in the garden – a hive with a sea of leaves surrounding it. What we see in our imagination is a complex image of the activity surrounding an aircraft carrier; the armed fighter planes are speeding up from their protective base and from the waves, their 'stings' ready for the enemy, but some will fall, their wings vanishing through the water. This war-elegy is echoed in a work under the little trees

beside the Temple Pool – a ceramic funerary urn with simple lettering:

OHKA
CHERRY BLOSSOM

First the aircraft type which Japanese suicide bomber pilots flew, then the sobriquet by which they were known in Japan at that time, cherry blossom: short-lived and beautiful.

The heroic tragedy and destruction condensed in this fleeting image is embodied too in a work commemorating the heavy cruiser *Minneapolis* of the US Navy, which was beached on a small island in the Pacific during the war. While repairs were done the need for camouflage was met by festooning it with the tropical foliage which grew on the island. The huge ship, powerful and alien, disguised itself, assuming an unremarkable appearance in keeping with the unfamiliar surroundings. With an illuminating leap of the imagination the ship becomes divine and able to maintain its power for redemption or for destruction unnoticed.

HABITARUNT DI QUOQUE SILVAS
EVEN GODS HAVE DWELT IN WOODS

The words from Virgil's pastoral *Eclogue III* endow the latter-day visitation of modern gods with mysterious dignity and, in contrast to the other visitation to Baucis

and Philemon, the outcome of the US warship's presence in the island waters takes on a more sombre aspect.

Certain Japanese military planes in the Pacific theatre of war were given code names by the Americans, and some of these are listed on a stone memorial tablet with the dates of their operations:

PETE

1936 – 1945

KATE

1937 – 1945

ZEKE

1937 – 1945

DINAH

1938 – 1943

JILL

1941 – 1945

The small-town American names and nicknames with the stark dates of their 'lives' take on a classical stature from the stele shape of the stone.

The use of ships in garden ornamentation, well established in classical Rome, is more familiarly known now from the Renaissance gardens of Italy, such as those of the Villa Lante and the Villa d'Este, where classical war galleys are incorporated in elaborately formal schemes of canals and

fountains. In the less grandiose setting of Little Sparta, the ships are on a smaller scale, but are perhaps more charming and certainly more thought-provoking. The Roman Garden, a shady, brick-paved corner of the Front Garden, contains a collection of stone ships in homage to the Villa d'Este, all small in scale, set on plinths to emphasize their status as monuments and semi-abstract in style. Nosing its way between a sea of green hosta plants in pots, *Nautilus*, an American nuclear-powered submarine, insinuates the idea of tremendous force contained in a sleekly designed vessel of destruction. A British aircraft carrier in a clearing of fir trees attracts the garden birds to its surface; the lifts which brought the aircraft up on deck from the depths of the ship have been transformed into little bird-baths filled with water, from which the birds can take off again to continue their raiding. Another carrier is represented only by its massive central funnel, and given the title *Carrier Torso* to shift our perception of its shape and function by the suggestion of classical sculpture of heroic nudes.

Corvettes were small ships in service with the British Navy and used to escort Atlantic convoys during the

Second World War. One class of these ships was named after flowers, and by their names alone these Flower class ships present a poignant paradox in the equation between the fragile, passing beauty of the flowers and the valour of the embattled men and vessels. Finlay uses this idea in three different works. First in a series of three plaques set into the drystone wall of the Front Garden which describe three Flower class corvettes lost in the Atlantic, one in the Free French Navy and the others British. The white lettering of the first reads:

A DRIFT
OF ALYSSE
ENG. Alyssum:
FLOWER CLASS CORVETTE
TORPEDOED 1942
W. ATLANTIC

The words on the second, actually the caption to a photograph in the book *Flower Class Corvettes* by Preston and Raven, evoke an image of flowers laid side by side, perhaps on a grave:

1942
TWO
FLOWERS
TO
GETHER
LOOSESTRIFE
PINK

With an inescapable irony in the name of the first. The third inscription is:

LOOSESTRIFE
6 SINGLE 20MM MOUNTS
PLUS A TWIN 20MM MOUNT
IN PLACE OF THE 2PDR POM-POM

A two-pounder pom-pom was a quick-firing anti-aircraft gun, but the *Loosestrife* had the eight gun mounts as its blossoms. Loosestrife is a particularly invasive plant.

Several Flower class corvettes were given by the British Navy to the American on the entry of the US into the war and the Americans renamed the ships in accordance with their ideals and temperament. A stone obelisk on an inscribed plinth in the English Parkland sadly commemorates this change:

Veronica became Temptress
Hibiscus became Spry
Arabis became Saucy
Periwinkle became Restless
Calendula became Ready
Begonia became Impulse
Larkspur became Fury
Heartsease became Courage
Candytuft became Tenacity

High on the edge of the moorland seven brick plinths are lined up, their bronze cappings and silhouetted corvettes catching the light. Each has a title and two of the plinths show the title of the whole series and the names of the ships. The series is called *Camouflaged Flowers* and the names are:

*VERLEAND   INCOMAP   YUPSHONALT
TIMENATOBR   TEGARBMO*

*LAVENDER   CAMPION   POLYANTHUS
MONTBRETIA BERGAMOT*

Which is camouflaged, flower or ship? The notion of flowers masquerading as ships in some sort of magical child's game collides with the image of the ships – with childlike trustfulness – believing themselves to be hidden behind their innocent names, and the two ideas are subsumed in the knowledge that there was nothing childlike or innocent in the reality of the corvettes' service.

The path from *Camouflaged Flowers* winds down from the edge of the moors to the banks of Lochan Eck where a polished black slate monolith rises from a low brick platform. Its surface is smoothly rounded with no angles or hard edges. The plaque at its foot reads:

NUCLEAR SAIL

Sail – a word whose very sound, as well as its associations, brings to mind peaceful, beautiful and harmless sea-going vessels. But instead of the slender, billowing elegance of a canvas sail this one's shape is as the conning tower, or sail, of a nuclear submarine rising here from the earth, its colour recalling the black sail of a ship bearing news of death. Its abstracted simplicity recalls the *Carrier Torso* in the Roman Garden, but in this context it is with an ironic, questioning reference to the work of sculptors such as Barbara Hepworth.

REVOLUTION

The French Revolution with its repertoire of terror, pastoralism, pathos and nostalgia for a Roman sense of republican honour provides a sublime metaphor and a many-faceted exemplar for Finlay's imagination to deploy. The Revolution's neoclassical sense of discipline and dignity pervades the series of tree-column bases in the garden. These are works whose apparent minimalism belies the monumental nature of their meaning. They are stone bases, like the bases of classical columns, that suggest simple Doric or Ionic orders rather than being of any flamboyant style. Where the stone column would rise a tree has been planted, too slender at first for the base, but in time destined to fill its proper space. Here is a set of implications to be contemplated: the natural and beautiful tree as the precursor of, or perhaps the model for, the more permanent stone column which will be fashioned with skill and diligence; the column as the essential support of a building as well as its embellishment; and the tree as the living inheritance from the achievements of the past. The men whose examples are honoured by the carving of their names on the tree bases are Rousseau, Corot, Michelet, Robespierre and Saint-Just, the first four set together among other trees, suggesting a sacred grove, a living temple to the ideals enshrined in their names. Saint-Just stands in the Front Garden, beside a stone planter carved

with the name *FABRE D'EGLANTINE* and containing an eglantine rose. Between them these six names evoke diverse aspects of the Revolution to engage our thoughts.

Camille Corot, born in 1796, expressed in his work the romantic feeling for the countryside that had been common to all the Revolutionaries. His sketches and paintings catch the play of light and shadow, the flickering changes in the movement of foliage. If there are figures in his landscapes they are usually mythical or, one might say, Arcadian. In him a certain Revolutionary spirit lingered.

Jules Michelet, born in 1798, wrote with deep emotion as well as intellectual insight a *History of the French Revolution*, which he felt to represent the victory of true justice over the oppressive corruption of the Christian Church and the institution of monarchy.

Jean-Jacques Rousseau's writings combine a tender sensibility towards the free expression of human emotions and relationships alongside passionate belief in republicanism and the existence of a quasi-divine spirit of guidance behind it. He promoted the ideals of justice, liberty and equality, of respect and affection for the countryside and its simple life, and his ideas underpinned much of republican thought. When he died in 1778 he was (temporarily) buried on the little Isle of Poplars in a lake on the estate of his protector the Marquis de Girardin, who contrived a tour of his park which led the visitor through romantic landscapes evocative of Rousseau's works and ideas to the island tomb. All this is evoked in turn by the tree plaque on an islet in the Upper Pool at Little Sparta entitling it *L'Ile des Peupliers*.

Maximilien Robespierre was a leader of the Jacobins, the political club which evolved ideals of freedom throughout the social structure of the state. His absolute devotion to liberty was matched by his conviction that a single will was needed to sweep aside irresolution and misplaced laxity of thought. This found expression in his adherence to the Reign of Terror's executions which he

nevertheless insisted should be just and necessary. Like Rousseau he believed in the existence of a God and tried to establish a cult of the Supreme Being. Attempting to create a civic religion which would inspire the people, in his role as president of the National Convention he led the Festival of the Supreme Being in the garden of the Tuileries in June 1794, but, undermined by ill health and increasingly beset by political enemies, he lost his grip on power and later that summer, caught up in the hysteria of the Terror, he was guillotined, along with Saint-Just and others. Robespierre has a touching memorial in the form of a painted metal watering can, an artefact essential to any garden, real or imaginary. Painted on it are his name and the dates of his life, which ended on the day called Arrosoir – watering can – in the republican calendar.

Louis Antoine de Saint-Just, guillotined before his twenty-seventh birthday, shared with Robespierre a single-minded devotion to the liberation of the French people from oppression and corruption. He spoke and wrote in passionately uncompromising terms about the absolute need to adhere to the good and extirpate the bad, and was even more extreme than Robespierre in his insistence on Terror as the weapon of virtue.

Philippe Fabre added d'Eglantine to his name when he claimed a golden eglantine rose as his prize in a literary competition. In 1793 he was given the task of renaming the months and days of the republican calendar which was to replace the Gregorian. His poetic choice of names reflected the pastoral and bucolic spirit of the Revolution, so that months acquired descriptive names such as Pluviôse, the rainy month, and Thermidor, the month of heat. Days too took on an aspect of country life with such names as Arrosoir, watering can, while the old saints' days took on names of trees and flowers. Despite these inspirational innovations Fabre was guillotined in 1794 at Robespierre's instigation because of his too-moderate views.

Marking progress along the path to the Upper Pool are four moulded cement baskets of fruit, nuts, plants and crayfish, brought together in the manner of architectural ornamentation. They are the names of days in the month of Fructidor, the beginning of the harvest time. The new months were divided into ten-day cycles, not seven-day weeks, with every fifth day given the name of an animal or fish which was part of the working life of the country and every tenth the name of an agricultural implement. So here Crayfish and Basket, while the other days are Eglantine, Hazelnut, Hops, Sorghum, Orange, Goldenrod, Maize and Chestnut.

Another Jacobin member of the Committee of Public Safety, guillotined alongside Robespierre and Saint-Just, was Georges Couthon, an ex-advocate whose body was twisted and paralysed by illness. He too has a monument at Little Sparta in the English Parkland, a section cut from a pure white serpentine column. Classical restraint and dignity are embodied in this poignant representation of his deformity and moral stature.

The deaths of the leading Jacobins in 1794, in the month of Thermidor, or late July, marked the downfall of the pure and ruthless revolution in favour of moderation and compromise. This is commemorated by a classical funerary urn on a brick plinth, bearing only the date.

Placed in a straight line between the house and the Temple Pool are four stone columns, each with a single inscription: *Liberty Equality Eternity 1793*. The change from the familiar slogan and the inclusion of the date point to the moment when the Committee of Public Safety succeeded in passing a resolution making terror the instrument of safeguarding the Revolution, so that

thousands found eternity at the guillotine rather than fraternity in the new society.

The largest work in the garden is up on the heathery moor and seen first from a path above it. Eleven huge, half-dressed blocks of stone lie in rows on the ground, each with a word carved on the top surface:

THE PRESENT ORDER IS THE DISORDER OF THE FUTURE SAINT-JUST

The heroic size of the blocks and their apparent existence as parts of some great building from which they have been either spirited or brutally wrenched away give them an aura of dreadful momentousness. The attribution of the judgement to Saint-Just and the implication of his importance as one whose sentiments are to be carved so strikingly in stone draw attention to the sternly Revolutionary intention of the words in condemnation of a corrupt society. Conversely and more disturbingly still we can see that although the blocks have been set out in this order they could be rearranged to give the opposite meaning. Here is a work which encapsulates Finlay's ability to see and express the idea of conflict as a crucial process, or perhaps more accurately as the moment when something new can be seen with explosive clarity. It may be a political imperative, a moral necessity or a point at which whatever makes us fully human demands a new response from us.

A final elegy on the Revolution and its doomed pursuit of an ideal is a simple stone block on the path in front of the house. The inscription on its face is adapted from Ovid's account in the *Metamorphoses* of the nymph Daphne's flight from her obsessed lover Apollo:

AND EVEN AS SHE FLED
THE REPUBLIC CHARMED HIM
THE WIND BLEW HER GARMENTS
AND HER HAIR STREAMED LOOSE
SO FLEW THE YOUNG REVOLUTI
ONARY AND THE SHY REPUBLIC
HE ON WINGS OF LOVE
AND SHE ON THOSE OF FEAR

The image of Daphne immortalized yet unfulfilled and Apollo uncomprehendingly frustrated leads us back to this most tragic of revolutions with its pure ideals and passionate, blind fanaticism. On the back of the block a further inscription gives a bibliography for the work: traditionally, bibliographies were often attached to emblems both to elucidate the text or image factually and to add a certain ambience. Here it reads:

OVID The Metamorphoses
Book I Fable XII IPOTESI
Saint-Just et l'Antiquité
PATER Apollo in Picardy
WITTKOWER Bernini
MIGNET Histoire de la Révolution Française

ART AND LITERATURE

Primarily a poet and concerned with words as sounds and visual signifiers as well as vehicles of meaning, Finlay also has an artist's eye and draws on his regard for earlier artists as the starting point for many works in the garden. By seeing the constructs of his landscapes in terms of another artist's interpretation of nature he draws us to consider what is art and what is nature – what is it that we perceive and understand when we look at the world, and how can an artist reinvent for us an aspect of the natural world.

The critic Erwin Panofsky suggested that for Western civilization Virgil invented the evening, in that he evoked something always there but not yet translated into an image which caught and fixed the special quality of evening-ness, the peace tinged with both melancholy and contentment. Finlay's comment on this Virgilian achievement is in a work consisting of a line of bricks with the word *Virgil* stamped into each one, stretching from the base of a tree over the grass, as an evening shadow.

Affectionate homage to great artists of the past appears in other works too. Thus on an island of turf in the Temple Pool, surrounded by grasses and wildflowers, is a stone tablet carved with the initials *AD* in the manner of Albrecht Dürer's monogram. So his *Great Piece of Turf* is

realized at our feet as at the same time the watercolour springs into our mind, and the circle of art, nature and imitation is complete. Dürer's monogram appears again on a little stone plaque fastened to the branch of a tree by a leather thong, as it is in his painting of Adam and Eve in their garden.

By the side of the Upper Pool, across the still, flag-fringed water from a little island containing a white marble tomb set among rushes and saplings, there is a stone obelisk, of more or less human height. Its inscription reads: *Il riposo di Claudio.* In the words of the eighteenth-century landscape theorist Uvedale Price, this refers to the peacefulness of Claude, the sense of calm beauty striven after by the landscape gardeners of the eighteenth century in their compositions of water, foliage and depth of view. This still, classical perfection imbues the landscapes of Claude Lorrain, often incorporating a tomb or distant buildings as well as an event of tragic import. The use of Italian as the shadow of Latin adds its antique note. The words might also be taken as the final rest of Claude, the obelisk as his monument linking one's perceptions to the tomb on the island opposite, bearing the carved words:

SILVER CLOUD
'standing out to sea'

SILVER CLOUD
'becalmed'

SILVER CLOUD
'towing'

SILVER CLOUD
'tacking in a light wind'

SILVER CLOUD
'sheet a' weather'

SILVER CLOUD
'full sail'

SILVER CLOUD
'dried out'

which are all taken from captions to photographs in a classic book on sailing drifters by Edgar J. Marsh. The boat name, allying the gleam of silver to the purity of the white marble, recalls the skies in paintings such as Claude's and stands for the beautiful perfection of his achievement, while the attributes open the way for a meditation on phases of human life.

A little stone tablet near by with the words

See POUSSIN
Hear LORRAIN

recalls another feature of Claude's paintings, the stirring of leaves by the wind made so striking visually that the

audible whispering comes to mind. At the same time we see here a scene of classical stillness, with marble monuments separated by a sheet of water, a scene that could be stolen from a painting by Poussin. The eighteenth-century Picturesque school, which contrived 'naturalness' in garden design by the introduction of such elements as rotting trees or tumbledown buildings, finds a lighthearted comment at the far corner of Lochan Eck, where the broken remnant of an old wooden fence leans down to the water's edge. Carved into one of its struts is the single word *PICTURESQUE*.

In the heart of the garden, sheltered from the moorland winds at the edge of the Temple Pool, where the pond plants luxuriate and birdsong fills the air around the overhanging trees, a plinth with a bronze plaque affixed to it carries a paragraph taken from a gallery brochure:

> *An oil painting by HORNEL dated 1918*
> *entitled THE BIRD'S NEST measuring*
> *14″ × 19″ has been made available for*
> *sale through the Demarco Gallery. The*
> *painting shows two small girls with*
> *bird's nest in foreground with blossom and*
> *two swans in background beside a stream.*

The blending of Japanese pattern and colour with Edwardian south-west Scottish landscape in Hornel's paintings of sylvan or pastoral scenes, often with children, sums up a nostalgia for the innocence of childhood and its secure place in the natural, bountiful garden of an unpolluted countryside. That nostalgia is underlined by our removal from the painting which we imagine through the medium of the unemotional announcement, excised from its context and placed in a setting which could appear in Hornel's work.

A very different artist is celebrated by a work near the entrance to the Front Garden, a rusticated stone base, not in this case for a tree, but a thistle, one of the large, prickly Scottish variety with many projecting leaves and triumphant flower heads. Its inscription is the artist's name – Piranesi, the Italian famous for his scenes of gigantic, complicated and menacing architecture, but perhaps less well known for the prickliness of his temper!

In many parts of the garden the works and their settings invite meditation and imaginative reflection, and this in turn invites solitude and quiet. The most overtly meditative corner of the garden is a little path leading from the Roman Garden through a grove of fir trees to an open stretch of lawn. There are three plinths spaced

out along the path, tall enough for their plaques to be read without stooping. They each carry a quotation from *The Mount of Olives, or Solitary Devotions,* a work of the Early Church Fathers translated from Latin by the seventeenth-century Anglo-Welsh metaphysical poet Henry Vaughan, whose deeply religious perceptions of nature and man dominated his writing:

> *The Contemplation of* death *is an obscure melancholy* walk
> *An* expatiation *in* shadows *and* solitude
> *But it leads unto* life

As in the sense of the texts the path leads out of the darkness of the conifer grove and into the light. In another part of the garden set under trees at the edge of a grassy corner there is a grey slate in the shape of a gravestone with a single sigla above the name and dates of Henry Vaughan. It stands as a restrained but deeply moving memorial and homage to Vaughan, using the sigla, an abbreviation or symbol, with which he marked a poem written as an elegy for a friend.

Under the trees which grow quite densely beside the Temple Pool, next to the path made from flagstones and bricks, there are three more plinths with inscriptions to

reverberate in the mind. They are quotations from the *Holzwege* of the twentieth-century German philosopher Martin Heidegger, describing the paths chopped out by woodcutters as they try to find ways through the forest:

> *In the woods*
> *are paths*
> *which mostly*
> *wind along*
> *until they end*
> *quite suddenly*
> *in an*
> *impenetrable thicket.*
>
> *They are called*
> *woodpaths.*
>
> *Often it seems*
> *as though one*
> *were like another,*
> *yet it only seems so.*

In his writings Heidegger deals with the meaning of *being,* and discusses emotions, behaviour and perceptions as philosophical topics. His work evolved from his love of the

Greek philosophers, particularly the pre-Socratics, and their use of metaphor and paradox, methods much used in his turn by Finlay. Finlay's installation of Heidegger's metaphor in a real wood, one of the secluded and most potentially solitary places in the garden, prompts the mind to move away from the real to the imagined, perhaps to Dante's dark wood, and the paths that we cut to discover ideas and feelings.

Moving from the sombrely reflective to the romantic, and Julie's Garden, we can find three trees there each with a ceramic plaque attached. The three pairs of names they bear are:

> *ROSALIND ORLANDO*
> *OENONE PARIS*
> *ANGELICA MEDORO*

– three pairs of lovers from the myth and literature of England, Greece and Italy, who fondly carved each other's names on trees, and whose tragedies and passions are recalled by this typically condensed work. In Shakespeare's *As You Like It* the Forest of Arden is the setting for the two exiles, Rosalind disguised as a boy, to find their way to happiness. In the *Heroides* Ovid tells of Oenone, a nymph of the Trojan hills who was loved by Paris, the shepherd and as yet unrecognized prince of Troy; but he abandoned her in favour of the Greek queen Helen; Oenone had the power of prophecy, and knew that his foray into Greece would bring disaster, but that Paris would return to her wounded and on the point of death. Angelica was adored by Orlando, the hero of Ariosto's mediaeval epic *Orlando Furioso,* but she fell in love with and married Medoro, a humble but beautiful boy, so that Orlando became mad with grief. Lovers still carve names, or hearts and arrows with initials on trees, and this tender practice has been much celebrated in the art and literature of the West. Here the artist abstracts the idea to create a classicizing accolade, transforming the rough carving into elegant yet still informal lettering on ceramic plaques and thereby suggesting that the trees have the potential to be columns.

There are two drystone wall works in the English Parkland. The sheep fank, or fold, with the text

> *ECLOGUE*
> *FOLDING*
> *THE LAST*
> *SHEEP*

on stone tablets, draws on the work of Samuel Palmer, the nineteenth-century follower of William Blake who, near the end of his life, translated Virgil's *Eclogues,* illustrating them with drawings and etchings of English pastoral scenes which are at once tender and charged with a visionary intensity.

The Gaelic text on the 'excerpt' from a long wall shows the resonant words of the bard Donald MacDonald of South Uist, born in 1926, included in Timothy Neat's book *The Voice of the Bard*:

> 'SE TOISEACH IS DEIREADH AN DUINE A'
> BHUACHAILLEACHD

The other side of the wall shows the text in English:

> THE BEGINNING AND THE END
> OF LIFE IS HERDING.

EVERYTHING IN THE GARDEN

Ideas in the garden can come from reveries, from fortunate coincidences and from the sheer pleasure afforded by the plants and paraphernalia of gardening. Finlay's wit and sense of fun have inspired many jokes and *jeux d'esprit*, not always untinged by sadness or seriousness, but always retaining a lightness and openness of spirit.

A stone bench in the Front Garden is inscribed with three items of *rose lore*:

> *THERE IS NO ROSE WITHOUT A THORN –*
> *THE FISHING LINE*
> *LIFE IS NOT ALL A BED OF ROSES –*
> *THE PARSLEY*
> *A ROSE IS A ROSE IS A ROSE –*
> *THE WATERING CAN*

The fishing line, the parsley and the watering can somehow acquire personalities, claiming the aphorisms for themselves with varying notes of wryness.

The American poet Gertrude Stein's dictum *a rose is a rose is a rose* appears elsewhere in the garden, this time on a ceramic watering can with the name of her contemporary *Gertrude Jekyll* added, conflating the literary association with the horticultural.

Another watering can made of painted metal has the words *Tea-Kettle-Drum Water-Lily-Cup* in contrasting

colours. Images of domestic tea parties, military fife and drum bands marching, drumming water falling on thirsty plants, delicate porcelain tea cups and water lilies holding crystalline drops of water crowd round, yet attain a balance and sense of controlled delight.

At one time geese were kept on Lochan Eck at Little Sparta, as in the simplest days of the Republic the Romans kept geese in the Capitol. In book five of his *History*, Livy describes how their cackling and flapping at night alerted the sleeping Romans to a surprise Gallic invasion. In the sometimes embattled domain of Little Sparta, a hut was built to house the geese at night; this hut, consisting of a wooden framework thatched with heather from the moor, follows a drawing by the eighteenth-century French architectural theorist Marc-Antoine Laugier,

Right A wild stone on the edge of the moor, whose carved words *CURFEW curlew* assign a new role to the curlew.

who advocated rationalism and simplicity in architecture, using the primitive hut as the shelter ideally suited to our needs.

The variety of bird life at Little Sparta reflects its richness of habitat in the setting of the moors. Curlews cry, moorhens scuttle into the reeds, ducks upend themselves to feed in the lochan, black swans with fluting calls move over the water, doves flutter and swoop and scores of small birds flit from tree to tree. In the crook of a rowan tree near the Roman Garden Finlay has placed one of the few works without words. It is a stone bird's nest with marble eggs inside, an utterly simple and charming work which gives monumental status to the vulnerable nest and at the same time produces the thrill of protective pleasure that we feel when we find a real nest in our gardens. Close by the bird's nest a slate tablet carries a concrete poem alerting us to the sound of the wind in the trees:

SONG	WIND	WOOD-
WIND	SONG	WIND
WOOD	WOOD	SONG

Read vertically the first two columns move the elements of the poem around, resolving them in the third; but the poem should also be read horizontally and diagonally, or even randomly to draw out the variations on its theme and reflect the confusion of movement and sound that the wind in the trees produces.

Placed on a slender stone column rising from the Temple Pool there is another work without words. This is a paper boat made of white marble (it can be seen in the photograph on page 62). Instantly recognizable as the shape of paper boats made for children to sail down little streams and follow their progress past weeds and dangerous eddies, the simple perfection of the genre is elevated and matched by the pure white marble.

Near the Temple Pool, by the edge of the Woodland Garden there is a stone bench with a wintry inscription:

*SNOW. n. atmos-
pheric vapour
frozen in a crystal-
line form. BARK. n.
formerly any small
sailing ship.*

*BARK. n. the rind
or covering of the
trunk and branches
of a tree. SNOW. n.
vessel like a brig
with a trysail mast.*

Simply two nouns, each with two factual dictionary definitions, but made into a concrete poem which reveals and shifts images of floating snowflakes, small sailing ships, little boats, perhaps sailed by Greek heroes or by lovers drifting to the romantic island of Cythera, and the trees which become the hulls of ships. The shape of the poem on the bench creates its rhythm. The eye can follow each definition vertically or stray horizontally to another definition and still find connections of words and layers of meaning, like half-formed memories and half-forgotten ideas. As the bench suggests rest the poem suggests a pause to reflect. And reflection in another sense is the key to a slate bench beside the Upper Pool whose inscription reads:

DUCK-DABBLED
WILLOW-SWEPT
WIND-SCUFFED
GRASS-GIRT
CLOUD-CURVED

with the text also carved upside down – its reflection – so that the bench becomes a description of the pool as it is and as it reflects its surroundings.

In most gardens which have been the setting for children growing up there has usually been at least one little grave for a bird or animal, clumsily but lovingly created by juvenile hands. Who has not solemnly buried a small bird, found dead, or a pet hamster, or even more sad, the family cat? Stonypath has such a domestic tomb near the house.

HERE I REST
HERE I STAY
OUR CAT
1977 – 1993

HERE I REST
HERE I STAY
OUR CAT
1977 – 1993

The Finlay cat's epitaph has grand antecedents. It is a quotation from a letter written from Aosta, his birthplace, by the eleventh-century Archbishop of Canterbury St Anselm, a Scholiast renowned for his ontological proof of the existence of God. A more homely feeling enters the second line with the idiomatic Scottish use of the word 'stay' to mean reside as well as remain, so the cat is still, as it were, at home.

Few gardeners would choose to cosset and celebrate the dandelion, but in a corner of Julie's Garden, an idyllic spot in Little Sparta named after the heroine of Rousseau's Romantic novel *Julie ou La nouvelle Héloïse*, there is a stone planter with two round spaces for plants. They are filled

with dandelions, and the blue lettering on elegant 'ribbons' of metal which decorate the lichen-stained surface explains the work:

HORLOGE DE FLORE
LES HEURES   LES MINUTES

It is a clock! A clock that is only to be consulted when the dandelion heads are puffy and white, ready to divulge the time to those who wish to blow the seeds away. Its charm is enhanced by the use of French, which suggests perhaps that the planter's real home is in a painting by Watteau or Fragonard where Flora, goddess of flowers, might dally, and where ribbons and garlands would abound.

Stonypath, like any self-respecting country garden, has a vegetable plot, but it is made into a Vegetable Plot by three slate plaques attached to its wall recalling the practice and ideals of Epicurus:

ALLOTMENT n. a garden of Epicurus

LIVE UNKNOWN   E✱✱✱✱✱✱s*

*BLEST YOUTH. SET SAIL IN YOUR BARK
& FLEE FROM EVERY FORM OF CULTURE*
Epicurus

First the definition of allotment reminds us that Epicurus advocated calm acceptance of one's lot, whatever it was, then the disguised attribution of his famous dictum

advocating a life of modest obscurity exemplifies it with quiet humour, while the final quotation from one of his letters challenges the idea of high culture, but perhaps also at times of weeding and digging?

In the Woodland Garden there are two stone herms on either side of a path. The head of one is Epicurus and the other is Zeno, founder of the Stoic school of philosophy, who held that happiness was to be attained by subjecting one's will to the divine reason. The two heads gaze impassively at each other across the path, and a slight frisson may be felt as one passes between them, interrupting their confrontation.

Two apparently sinister stone tablets at opposite ends of the Front Garden turn out to be less serious than first impressions suggest.

ACHTUNG!
MINEN

warns one near the house; but this quotation, familiar from Second World War films if not from experience, of the German notices posted to warn trespassers away from mine fields, here alerts those who weed or dig that it marks the spot where the underground electricity cable enters the garden, so retreat is advisable.

BRING
BACK
THE
BIRCH

declares the other, on a tablet shaped like a Greek stele set before a copse of maples and hornbeams. Once again an old catchphrase is put to new use: it is not corporal punishment that is wanted, simply the natural birch trees of the moorland.

For those who feel in urgent need of a solitary place to hide, brood and sulk there is a double hedgerow with a path running between and five benches to encourage rest

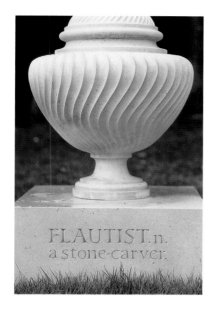

and reflection. This is Huff Lane, a retreat for the alienated. The inscriptions on the benches, to be remembered and pondered on the occasion of one's next huff, read:

The song of a skylark may return us to Shelley,
a lane may lead us back to Clare.

A lane need not meander.

A glimpse of the sea, the sound of a distant aeroplane open a
chink in the solitude of even the deepest lane.

A lane cannot be measured in metres.

In a lane one will not encounter Apollo,
but one may come upon Pan.

Emerging refreshed from Huff Lane we can see two musical works to lighten the heart even more. A stone urn on a plinth is delicately carved with fluting all round, and its title reads *FLAUTIST. n. a stone carver*, the pun as delicate as the work.

The second work is about fluting also, in another mode. A group of trees planted inside a circle of stone setts with a tablet in the middle celebrates the variety of the trees.

A WOODLAND FLUTE

BETULA

PENDULA

CARPINUS

BETULUS

VIBURNUM

OPULUS

POPULUS

TREMULA

PRUNUS

Silver Birch, Hornbeam,

Guelder Rose, Aspen, Plum

Set closely together the trees provide a changing mass of colours and sounds in the wind, but more than that – looking closely at the placing of the Latin names we can see that the U sounds follow each other down the list, as the finger holes in a flute follow down its length.

Perhaps the work one might want to see last before leaving the garden is one which encapsulates something of what Finlay has achieved at Little Sparta. Two circular plaques are placed in stone setts with lines from the fourth book of Virgil's *Georgics* spelt out on them:

Illi tiliae atque uberrima pinus
Quotque in flore novo pomis se fertilis arbos
Induerat totidem autumno matura tenebat

Ille etiam seras in versam distulit ulmos
Eduramque pirum et spinos iam pruna ferentis
Iamque ministrantem plantanum potantibus umbras

'He had lime trees and the most luxuriant pine, and every fruit his bountiful tree took on when first it blossomed it kept to ripeness in the autumn. He even transplanted well-grown elms in rows, and pear trees when they were hardened and thorns bearing sloes and a plane tree already giving shade to those who came to drink.'

Not only the horticultural transformation of moorland to garden is reflected in these lines, but also Finlay's mode of working as an artist. He draws on the art of the past, uprooting it and incorporating it into his own in a way that renews it and extends its meaning as it brings delightfully fresh perceptions to its audience. His immensely diverse stock of ideas and images ranges from the homely and familiar to the intellectually abstruse, and by what can only be called the magic of art he makes from them works to lift the spirit and touch the heart. Those who come prepared to find in Little Sparta works whose essence is poetic, not decorative or horticultural, will find subsequently that the way they see the world is changed and made more wonderful.

INDEX

VISITOR INFORMATION

Little Sparta, near the village of Dunsyre, some twenty-five miles south-west of Edinburgh, can be visited from June to September on Friday and Sunday afternoons.

Further information can be had by telephone to Little Sparta, 0189 981 0252, or from the Little Sparta Trust, which exists to support and conserve the garden. Donations to help with its work are welcome.

The Secretary
Little Sparta Trust
Auchenshore
Auchencairn
Castle Douglas
Galloway
DG7 1QZ

MUSCOSI FONTES ET SOMNO MOLLIOR HERBA
'Mossy springs and grass softer than sleep.'
Virgil, *Eclogue VII*

LEA NURSERY SCHOOL
WEXHAM ROAD
SLOUGH.

for

Patrick

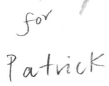

First published 2004 by Walker Books Ltd
87 Vauxhall Walk, London SE11 5HJ

2 4 6 8 10 9 7 5 3 1

© 2004 Clare Jarrett

The right of Clare Jarrett to be identified as
author/illustrator of this work has been asserted by her in
accordance with the Copyright, Designs and Patents Act 1988

This book has been typeset in Aunt Mildred

Printed in China

British Library Cataloguing in Publication Data:
a catalogue record for this book is available
from the British Library

ISBN 0-7445-9283-6

www.walkerbooks.co.uk

The Best Picnic Ever

Clare Jarrett

WALKER BOOKS
AND SUBSIDIARIES
LONDON · BOSTON · SYDNEY · AUCKLAND

One day Jack went to the park with his mum to have a picnic. While Mum made the picnic, Jack looked about.

"I wish there was someone to play with," said Jack.

"There is," said Giraffe. "Me!"

"Please come to our picnic," said Jack. "How kind," said Giraffe, "but first let's play."

"We'll gallop," said Giraffe.
"And whiz and whoosh," said Jack.
And while Mum made the picnic,

Jack and Giraffe went
gallopy, gallopy, gallopy through
the tall grass.

Then they met Elephant.
"That looks fun," he said.

"Come to our picnic," said Jack.
"How kind," said Elephant,
"but first let's play."

"Let's trumpet,"
said Elephant.
"And make a huge noise," said Jack.
And while Mum made the picnic,
Jack and Elephant went toot, toot,
toot, tootley-toot-toot, with Giraffe
going gallopy, gallopy, gallopy
through the tall grass behind them.

Then they met Leopard.
"What a great noise,"
he said.

"Come and join our picnic," said Jack.
"How kind," said Leopard,
"but first can we play?"

"Let's leap about," said Leopard.
"Great long lolloping leaps," said Jack.
And while Mum made the picnic,
Jack and Leopard went lollopy,

lollopy, lollopy, with Elephant going
toot, toot, toot, tootley-toot-toot and
Giraffe going gallopy, gallopy, gallopy
through the tall grass behind them.

Then they met Tiger.
"Come to our picnic,"
said Jack.
"How kind,"
said Tiger,
"but first
let's dance."

"And tap our toes," said Jack.
And while Jack and Tiger danced,
Leopard went lollopy, lollopy, lollopy
and Elephant went toot, toot, toot,
tootley-toot-toot and Giraffe went
gallopy, gallopy, gallopy behind them.
They tapped and lolloped and tooted
and galloped, faster and faster,
until they heard Mum say ...

"The picnic's ready!"

"Hurrah!" said everyone.

So they all went back to the
most delicious picnic.

There were sausages, pizza,
chocolate cake and strawberries.

Soon it was time to go home.
"Goodbye," said all the animals.
"Goodbye," said Jack. "And thank you,
everyone. That was the
best picnic ever!"